Archplot Structure

Explained

By Michelle Murray

Copyright © 2024 Michelle Murray

All rights reserved. This book or any portion thereof may not be reproduced or used in any manner whatsoever without the express written permission of the publisher except for the use of brief quotation in a book review.

Printed in the United States of America

KMP Entertainment (Publishing Division)
www.kmpentertainment.org

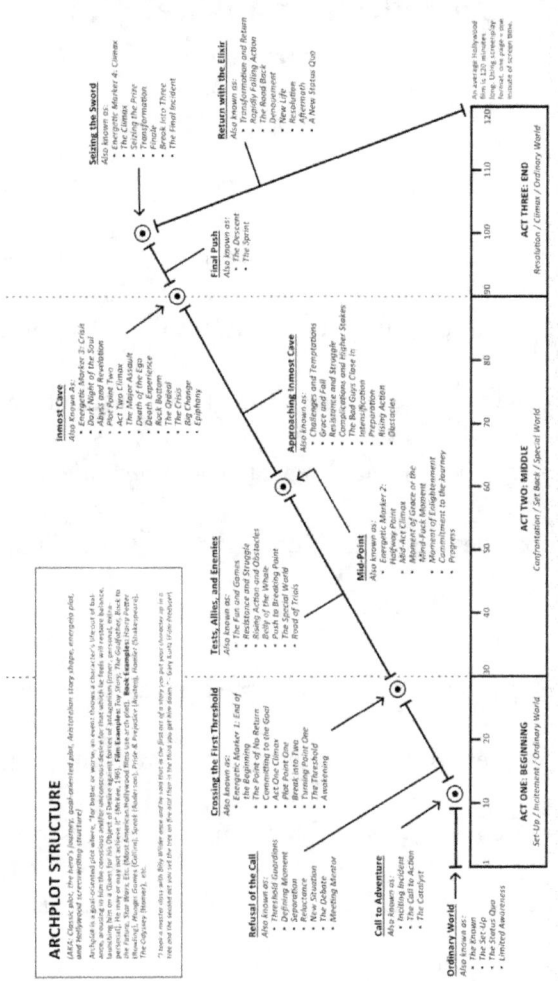

Introduction to Archplot Structure

As a writer, understanding the concept of archplot structure is crucial to crafting a compelling and engaging story. Archplot structure, also known as the three-act structure, is a widely used narrative framework that provides a strong foundation for storytelling. In essence, archplot structure is a blueprint that helps writers organize their ideas and plot progression in a logical and coherent manner. It consists of three main acts: setup, confrontation, and resolution. Each act serves a specific purpose and contributes to the overall development of the story.

The first act, the setup, is where the groundwork for the entire story is laid. It introduces the main characters, their goals, and the world they inhabit. This act sets the stage and establishes the status quo. By presenting the initial equilibrium or ordinary life of the protagonist, the setup creates a reference point against which the changes and challenges of the story will be measured. Within the setup, the inciting incident serves as a catalyst for the protagonist's journey.

It is an event or occurrence that disrupts the protagonist's ordinary life and propels them into action. The inciting incident often ignites conflict, raises questions, or presents opportunities that compel the protagonist to embark on their quest or face a pressing problem. This pivotal event hooks the readers, piquing their curiosity and drawing them deeper into the story. The setup should establish the basic elements of the story, including the setting, the tone, and the rules of the world in which the characters exist. By effectively presenting these foundational aspects, writers can create a believable and immersive narrative that captivates readers' imaginations.

The second act, the confrontation, is the longest and most eventful part of the narrative. It presents numerous challenges, conflicts, and obstacles that the protagonist must face and overcome. This act tests the protagonist's determination, skills, and character growth. It builds rising action and intensifies the story, leading to a climax or turning point. During the confrontation, the protagonist encounters a series of obstacles and setbacks that force them to adapt, learn, and evolve. These roadblocks can take various forms, such as external forces like villains, natural disasters, or societal pressures, or internal conflicts like self-doubt, emotions, or past traumas.

The complexity and variety of challenges contribute to the depth and richness of the story, ensuring readers remain engaged and invested in the outcome. In addition to challenges, the confrontation should also introduce conflicts that bring out the complexities of the main characters. These conflicts can arise from their relationships, beliefs, or contrasting desires. By exploring these internal and external conflicts, writers have the opportunity to delve into the depths of their characters and create multidimensional personalities that readers can identify with and root for. The confrontation intensifies as the protagonist faces increasingly difficult obstacles. The rising action builds suspense and tension, heightening the stakes and drawing readers deeper into the story. The conflicts may escalate to critical junctures, such as midpoint climaxes or major revelations, where the protagonist must make pivotal choices that significantly impact their journey.

The climax, also known as the midpoint, is the pivotal moment in the story where the protagonist's fortunes hang in the balance. It is the peak of tension and conflict, and it often forces the protagonist to make a crucial decision or take significant action. The climax propels the story toward its resolution. The climax serves as a turning point or a moment of truth for the protagonist. It can involve high-stakes confrontations, profound revelations, or powerful realizations that propel the narrative forward.

This critical juncture often brings to the surface the protagonist's strengths and weaknesses, forcing them to confront their deepest fears and make life-altering choices. The outcome of the climax will directly shape the rest of the story, leading to either triumph or defeat. The climax should provide a cathartic release for readers. It is the culmination of the tension and conflicts built throughout the confrontation. The stakes should be raised to a point where the resolution becomes highly anticipated, ensuring that readers are emotionally invested in the resolution of the story.

The third act, the resolution, brings about the conclusion of the story. It highlights the final confrontations, resolutions of conflicts, and the ultimate outcome for the protagonist. This act is where loose ends are tied up, lessons are learned, and the story reaches its climax in terms of emotional intensity.

The resolution often offers a sense of fulfillment or catharsis for readers. Within the resolution, various elements come together to provide a satisfying conclusion. The protagonist's growth and transformation, as well as the resolution of their main conflicts, serve as the primary focus, allowing readers to witness the fruits of the protagonist's journey. It is here that the protagonist's evolution is fully realized, and they confront the main antagonist or the central problem once and for all. Additionally, the resolution should offer closure, providing answers to the questions and conflicts raised throughout the narrative. Readers should feel a sense of actual resolution and satisfaction as they witness the "wrapping up" of subplots and the attainment of the protagonist's goals. However, it is important to strike a balance between providing closure and leaving room for readers' imagination and interpretation.

This balance ensures that readers feel a sense of completion while still being intellectually and emotionally engaged. The resolution often carries themes of redemption, sacrifice, or justice, depending on the nature of the story. It allows writers to deliver powerful messages, explore the consequences of actions, and provide moral resolutions that resonate with readers. The resolution should resonate with readers on a deeper level, leaving them with a sense of resonance and reflection.

While archplot structure provides a framework, it is important to note that writers have the freedom to deviate from it or add their unique twists and variations. The key is to understand the fundamental principles of storytelling and use archplot structure as a tool to strengthen the overall narrative. In the following chapters, we will delve deeper into the different elements and techniques involved in creating a compelling archplot structure. By mastering these techniques and understanding how they contribute to the story's impact, you'll be well-equipped to captivate your readers and craft a remarkable story.

Understanding the Fundamentals of Storytelling

Storytelling is a timeless art form that has captivated audiences throughout history. It is the vehicle through which writers can convey their ideas, evoke emotions, and create a deep connection with readers. So let's explore the fundamentals of storytelling in more depth and delve deeper into how they can be utilized to enhance your writing.

The Power of a Strong Narrative:

A compelling narrative is the backbone of any great story. It provides structure, engages readers, and keeps them invested in the journey. To develop a strong narrative, it is essential to consider the following elements:

Plot: The sequence of events that drive the story forward. A well-crafted plot incorporates elements such as exposition, rising action, climax, falling action, and resolution. These elements work together to create a cohesive and satisfying story arc. Additionally, consider incorporating subplots that intertwine with the main plot, adding layers of complexity and intrigue.

Characters: The key players in your story. Fully developed, relatable characters add depth and authenticity to your narrative. Give each character a unique voice, personality, and backstory that complements their role in the story. Pay attention to their motivations, goals, and conflicts, as these shape their actions and interactions throughout the story. By understanding your characters on a profound level, you can create rich, multidimensional individuals that readers can connect with and root for.

Setting: The environment in which your story takes place. A vividly described setting can transport readers to different worlds and immerse them in your story. It encompasses not only the physical aspects but also the cultural, historical, and social context of the world you are building. By paying attention to intricate details such as the geography, climate, and societal structures, you can make your setting come alive, creating a more immersive experience for readers.

Theme: The overarching message or idea that you want to convey through your story. Themes provide depth and meaning to your narrative, allowing readers to connect on a deeper level. Explore universal themes such as love, loss, identity, the human condition, or the consequences of power. By addressing these themes in various ways throughout your story, you can offer profound insights and invite readers to reflect on these concepts, fostering a thought-provoking experience.

Understanding the Audience

To create a compelling story, it is important to understand your audience. Consider their preferences, interests, and what they are looking to gain from reading your work. By understanding your target audience, you can tailor your storytelling techniques to better resonate with them. –

Genre Considerations: Different genres have specific storytelling conventions and expectations. Fantasy readers may seek immersive world-building and epic quests, while mystery enthusiasts enjoy clever plot twists and suspenseful narratives. Consider the genre conventions and reader expectations to ensure your story aligns with their preferences.

Emotional Connection: Consider the emotions you want to evoke in your readers. Whether it's joy, sadness, fear, hope, or a combination of these, emotional resonance is key to capturing their attention and creating a lasting impact. Craft your story in a way that elicits emotions through relatable characters, powerful conflicts, and thoughtfully constructed scenes. Create moments that tug at the heartstrings or push readers to reflect on their own experiences.

Writing Style: Understand your readers' preferences regarding writing style. Some audiences appreciate lyrical prose while others enjoy straightforward and concise storytelling. Tailor your writing style to engage your audience and create an immersive experience for them. Experiment with different techniques, such as imagery, figurative language, or experimental narrative structures, to further enhance your storytelling prowess.

Creating Engaging Characters

Characters are the driving force behind any story. Readers connect with characters who feel real and experience a range of emotions with them. When developing your characters, consider the following aspects:

Motivations: Understand your characters' motivations for their actions and choices. What drives them? Is it love, revenge, or the pursuit of a higher purpose? By grounding their motivations in their core desires, values, and beliefs, you can create more authentic characters that resonate with readers.

Flaws: Flawed characters are relatable and resonate with readers. Examine their weaknesses, fears, and insecurities. These flaws not only add depth and complexity but also provide growth opportunities for your characters. Allow them to grapple with their flaws and learn from their mistakes, showcasing their resilience and capacity for change.

Relationships: The dynamics between characters play a significant role in storytelling. Whether it's friendship, romance, rivalry, or familial bonds, explore how relationships affect your characters and propel the plot forward. Develop these relationships with nuance and authenticity, allowing readers to invest in the connections and experience the emotional impact.

Character Arcs: Ensure that your characters experience personal growth and change throughout the story. A well-constructed character arc allows readers to witness their transformation, fostering empathy and investment in their journey. As your characters face challenges, conflicts, and learn valuable lessons, let their experiences shape them into who they become by the end of the story.

Crafting an Effective Narrative Structure

A well-structured narrative provides a clear and satisfying reading experience. Consider using storytelling techniques such as:

Introduction: Grab readers' attention from the beginning by introducing your characters and their world. Set the stage for the story to come, enticing readers with hints of what's to come. Use descriptive language and engaging details to paint a vivid picture of the setting, instantly immersing readers in the story.

Conflict: Create tension and obstacles that your characters must overcome, driving the story forward. Incorporate both external conflicts (such as fighting against a villain or facing a natural disaster) and internal conflicts (such as battling inner demons or moral dilemmas). These conflicts provide opportunities for growth, development, and transformation.

Climax: The peak of the story where the conflict reaches its highest point, leading to a significant change or resolution. This is the point where all the elements of your story come together for a powerful impact. The climax should be intense, dramatic, and emotionally charged, leaving readers on the edge of their seats as they witness the decisive moment that determines the fate of the characters.

Falling Action: After the climax, gradually wind down the tension and allow your characters to reflect on their experiences. Provide necessary information for a satisfying resolution. Use this phase of the story to tie up loose ends, answer lingering questions, and offer closure to readers. Though the pace may slow down, ensure that every scene serves a purpose in furthering character development or enhancing the overall narrative.

Resolution: Tie up loose ends and provide closure for your readers. Ensure that all major plot points are addressed, and conflicts are resolved. However, it's important to strike a balance between providing closure and leaving room for readers' imagination.

Consider leaving some aspects open-ended or hinting at new beginnings, allowing readers to ponder the potential futures of the characters beyond the final pages of your story.

Utilizing Pacing and Tension

Pacing is crucial to maintain reader engagement. A well-balanced mix of fast-paced and slower moments creates a rhythm that keeps readers hooked. Varied pacing can create tension, keeping readers on the edge of their seats. Consider the following techniques:

Action Scenes: Inject moments of high energy and excitement within tense action scenes. These scenes should be fast-paced and filled with adrenaline. Use dynamic and vivid language to describe the action, making readers feel as if they are right in the middle of the action. Shorter sentences and paragraphs can enhance the sense of urgency and speed, while longer descriptions can slow down the pace and allow readers to catch their breath.

Suspense and Foreshadowing: Keep readers engaged by creating a sense of anticipation and suspense. Foreshadow future events through subtle hints and clues, building tension and intrigue. Delay the revelation of important information, allowing readers to speculate and form theories about what is going to happen. Use cliffhangers at the end of chapters or scenes to leave readers wanting more and eager to continue reading.

Emotional Intensity: Emotional intensity can also contribute to the pacing and tension of a story. Intense emotional scenes, such as confrontations, revelations, or moments of deep reflection, can create a powerful effect on readers. Use vivid and evocative language to capture the emotional turmoil experienced by your characters, immersing readers in their emotional journey.

Time and Structure: The manipulation of time and the structure of your story can also impact pacing and tension. By alternating between past and present, or by using flashbacks and flash-forwards, you can create a sense of suspense and keep readers guessing. Additionally, varying the length and structure of chapters and scenes can add variety to the pace of your story, preventing it from becoming monotonous.

Evoking Emotion Through Descriptive Writing

Descriptive writing is a powerful tool for engaging readers and evoking emotions. By using vivid language and sensory details, you can create a deep connection between readers and your story. Consider the following techniques:

Show, Don't Tell: - Instead of simply telling readers how characters feel or what the setting looks like, show it through descriptive writing. Use strong and specific language to paint a vivid picture in readers' minds. Describe the physical sensations, smells, sounds, and tastes to fully immerse readers in the scene.

Imagery: Create strong mental images through descriptive language and vivid metaphors. Use sensory details to engage readers' senses and make your story come alive. For example, instead of saying "the flowers were beautiful," describe the colors, fragrance, and texture of the flowers in detail. This will allow readers to visualize the scene and experience it more fully.

Symbolism: Employ symbols and metaphors to add depth and meaning to your descriptions. Symbolism can create a deeper emotional impact and subtly convey themes and ideas. For example, the recurring image of a bird may symbolize freedom or a butterfly may symbolize transformation. Use symbols sparingly and with purpose, allowing readers to draw their own interpretations.

Tone and Mood: Consider the tone and mood you want to convey through your descriptions. Descriptions can vary from a romantic and lyrical tone to a dark and ominous tone, depending on the atmosphere you want to create. Use language, sentence structure, and metaphorical language to set the tone and immerse readers in the desired mood.

Sensory Details: Engage readers' senses by incorporating sensory details into your descriptions. Instead of just describing how a location looks, explore how it smells, sounds, and feels. This will create a more immersive experience for readers, allowing them to feel as if they are experiencing the story firsthand.

Authenticity: When describing emotions or experiences, be authentic and true to the character's perspective. Put yourself in their shoes and think about how they would perceive and describe things. This will create a more genuine and relatable experience for readers. By utilizing these storytelling fundamentals, you can enhance the impact of your writing, engage readers, and create compelling and memorable stories. Remember to experiment, be open to feedback, and continuously develop your storytelling skills to become a masterful storyteller.

Crafting a Strong and Memorable Protagonist

In every great story, a compelling and relatable protagonist is the backbone of the narrative. It is the protagonist who captures the attention of readers and guides them through the journey of the story. Crafting a strong and memorable protagonist requires careful thought and consideration, as this character will carry the weight of the entire plot. To create a protagonist that resonates with readers, it is essential to first understand their motivations and goals.

What drives them? What do they want to achieve? These questions lay the foundation for a well-rounded and believable character. For example, consider a protagonist who desires wealth and power. Is their motivation rooted in a difficult childhood where they experienced poverty and powerlessness?

By understanding the protagonist's motivations on a profound level, you can infuse their desires with emotional weight, allowing readers to connect with their aspirations and feel invested in their journey. Memorable protagonists go beyond mere desires.

They must be three-dimensional, with strengths, weaknesses, and flaws that make them relatable and human. While it can be tempting to create a flawless protagonist, remember that imperfections make characters more believable and relatable. These imperfections allow readers to connect with the character on a deeper level, as they can see themselves reflected in the struggle to overcome challenges and grow.

Imagine a protagonist who has a fear of failure. This fear drives them to constantly push themselves, but it also holds them back from taking risks. This flaw humanizes the protagonist and makes their accomplishments and growth more inspiring. Additionally, an essential aspect of creating a memorable protagonist is their emotional journey.

As the story progresses, the protagonist should experience growth, transformation, or a shift in perspective. This evolution adds depth and complexity to the character, making them more compelling and engaging for readers. Consider how the protagonist's emotions are impacted by their experiences, and how these emotional changes influence their decisions and actions. Does a tragedy lead them to question their beliefs? Does a moment of vulnerability force them to confront their fears?

By allowing readers to witness the protagonist's emotional journey, they become invested in the character's development, eagerly following them through the narrative. It is crucial to consider how the protagonist interacts with other characters and the world around them. Their relationships and conflicts should be richly developed, creating opportunities for growth and tension.

These interactions shape the protagonist's development and allow readers to witness their journey of self-discovery. By bringing the protagonist's relationships to life, readers gain insight into their values, vulnerabilities, and character. Characters that challenge the protagonist's beliefs or provide support and encouragement can create captivating dynamics that drive the narrative forward.

For example, a mentor who challenges the protagonist's worldview can create conflict that pushes them to reevaluate their assumptions, ultimately leading to growth. Fully developing a character plays a vital role in crafting a memorable protagonist. It is important to represent a range of backgrounds, and perspectives within our stories. Consider how your protagonist's identity and experiences are shaped by their background, gender, abilities or other things.

By integrating a variety of aspects into your character, you not only strengthen the authenticity of your protagonist but also expand the potential reach and impact of your story. When readers see themselves or something familiar within the protagonist, they can connect more deeply, empathize, and find inspiration. Remember to approach these details with accuracy, doing thorough research.

Crafting a strong and memorable protagonist requires a deep understanding of the motivations, desires, flaws, and growth of the character. It is through their journey that the story unfolds and captivates readers. Invest time and care in creating a protagonist that stands out, and your story will benefit from their compelling presence. Understand their desires and motivations, explore their flaws and vulnerabilities, depict their emotional journey, and create meaningful relationships. By doing these things, your protagonist will resonate with readers, leaving a lasting impression that ensures your story lives beyond

the pages of your script.

The Hero's Journey: Exploring the Stages and Significance

Now let's delve deeper into one of the most influential and widely recognized narrative structures in storytelling: The Hero's Journey. Joseph Campbell, a renowned scholar of mythology, examined various cultural myths and discovered a universal pattern that underlies the hero's journey. By understanding and incorporating these stages into your own writing, you can create compelling stories that resonate deeply with readers.

<u>The Call to Adventure:</u> The hero begins in the ordinary world, consumed by familiar routines and a sense of comfort. This initial stage introduces readers to the hero's character, establishing their desires, strengths, flaws, and aspirations. However, destiny intervenes, and the hero receives a call to embark on a quest or an adventure. This call may come from within, through a yearning for growth and change, or from an external source like a mentor figure, a supernatural being, or a prophetic dream. The call disrupts the hero's ordinary life and sets them on the path of the journey that will cause some change/growth by the story's end.

The Refusal of the Call: When the hero receives the call, they may initially refuse or resist it. Fear, self-doubt, or attachment to their mundane existence can create a reluctance to journey into the unknown. This refusal is crucial as it establishes the hero's vulnerability and sets the stage for their growth. It also allows readers to empathize with the hero's internal struggle and cheer for their eventual acceptance of the call. This refusal can be a result of the hero questioning their ability or worthiness, highlighting their human flaws and relatability to readers.

Meeting the Mentor: At this stage, the hero encounters a mentor figure who provides guidance, wisdom, and assistance. Mentors can take various forms, such as a wise old man, an experienced warrior, a supernatural being, or even a symbolic representation of the hero's own inner strength. The mentor equips the hero with the knowledge, tools, or skills required to navigate the challenges and tests they will face on their journey. Through their guidance and support, mentors empower the hero to tap into their true potential and face their fears with newfound confidence.

<u>Crossing the First Threshold:</u> After receiving guidance from their mentor, the hero takes a decisive step and crosses the first threshold, leaving behind their familiar world and entering a new and unfamiliar realm. This threshold can be a physical location or a symbolic representation of the hero's inner journey. Crossing the threshold can be accompanied by trials, tests, or obstacles that challenge the hero's resolve and commitment to their quest. These challenges serve to strengthen the hero's determination and readiness for what lies ahead. It is important to emphasize the significance of this threshold crossing as an irreversible commitment to the hero's transformative journey.

<u>Tests, Allies, and Enemies:</u> In the midst of the hero's journey, they encounter a series of trials, tests, or challenges. These challenges may manifest as physical obstacles, psychological barriers, or moral dilemmas. Through these experiences, the hero grows, gains new insights, and acquires essential skills or knowledge necessary to progress further.

Along the way, the hero forms alliances with other characters who become allies, providing support, guidance, or camaraderie. Conversely, the hero may also face adversaries who become enemies, acting as mirrors to reflect the hero's weaknesses or intensifying the stakes of their journey. These tests, allies, and enemies add depth to the hero's growth, highlighting their evolution as they navigate through various conflicts and obstacles.

The Approach to the Inmost Cave:

As the hero advances toward their ultimate goal, they approach a significant challenge or obstacle, often referred to as the "inmost cave." This can represent the hero's deepest fears, insecurities, or unresolved conflicts, whether external or within themselves. By facing this inner or outer obstacle, the hero undergoes a truly life changing experience, shedding old beliefs or behaviors and emerging stronger and more resilient than before. This stage can be pivotal in the hero's journey as they confront their darkest moments, confront their inner demons, and make choices that define their character.

<u>The Ordeal:</u> The "ordeal" is a climactic moment in the hero's journey when they face their greatest test or challenge. It is a moment of intense tension and uncertainty, where the hero's skills, resolve, and character are pushed to their limits. The hero must confront their deepest fears, make difficult choices, and perhaps even sacrifice something significant in order to overcome the ordeal. This pivotal moment forces the hero to confront their weaknesses, embrace their strengths, and undergo a profound change or revelation. The ordeal is a life changing experience that pushes the hero beyond their perceived limitations and solidifies their growth and.

The Reward: Upon overcoming the ordeal, the hero reaps a reward or achieves the initial goal they set out to accomplish. The reward can be tangible, such as an object or treasure, or intangible, such as knowledge, self-realization, or a heightened sense of purpose. This reward serves as a symbolic victory and reinforces the hero's growth and evolution. It may also empower the hero in further confronting future challenges. It is crucial, though, to emphasize that the reward is not the ultimate goal but rather a stepping stone toward the hero's ultimate transformation.

The Road Back: Having achieved their initial goal, the hero begins the journey back to their ordinary world. However, this road back may not be a smooth one. The hero may face one final obstacle or test, acting as a threshold between their transformative experience and their return to their previous life. This stage tests the hero's commitment and resolve, as they may experience temptation to abandon the journey or revert to their old ways. It is through this final ordeal that the hero demonstrates their unwavering dedication to their newfound purpose. The road back provides closure to the hero's transformative journey, showcasing their strength, growth, and the knowledge gained from their experiences.

The Resurrection: In this final stage, the hero faces a climactic showdown or confrontation, often with the antagonist or an embodiment of their inner conflict. The hero must confront and overcome their ultimate challenge, drawn from the depths of their being. The triumph in this moment goes beyond external victory; it signifies the hero's inner transformation and their emergence as a renewed individual. By conquering their own fears, the hero demonstrates their growth, resilience, and newfound understanding. The resurrection stage highlights the hero's ability to rise above their limitations and embrace their true potential.

<u>The Return with the Elixir:</u> The hero returns to their ordinary world, bringing with them the rewards, knowledge, or transformation gained from their journey. The elixir can be the physical manifestation of their quest, a newly gained wisdom, or an intangible gift that contributes to personal growth. This return serves as a conclusion to the hero's transformative journey, offering closure and providing a resolution to the story's conflicts.

The hero's return not only marks a personal triumph but also provides an opportunity to make a positive impact on their community or society. With their newfound wisdom, abilities, or perspective, the hero can now heal, inspire, or bring about positive change in the lives of others. Incorporating the stages of The Hero's Journey into your writing will add depth and resonance to your narrative. This framework serves as a guide that will aid you in creating the best story possible.

The Hero's Journey is not limited to epic fantasy or adventure genre stories. This narrative structure can be applied to a wide range of genres, including contemporary fiction, science fiction, mystery, and even nonfiction. By understanding the underlying principles of the Hero's Journey, you can craft compelling character arcs and visceral, impactful stories that resonate with the audience on a deep and emotional level. It is essential to make each stage of the Hero's Journey meaningful and significant. Each step should contribute to the hero's growth, reveal new insights, or create tension and conflict that fuels the story's momentum. Avoid treating the stages as mere checkboxes to be ticked off. Instead, focus on delivering engaging and memorable experiences for your readers. Don't limit the roles of the hero and the mentor to specific gender or age categories. The hero can be of any gender, age, or background, and the mentor can take various forms. What matters most is the dynamic between the two and the wisdom the mentor provides. The Hero's Journey is a timeless narrative structure that has stood the test of time because it taps into universal human experiences and desires. It captures the essence of personal growth and resilience, making it a powerful tool for storytelling. By understanding and utilizing this structure, you can create narratives that not only entertains but will inspire and connect with readers on an emotional level. So, embrace the hero's journey and embark on a storytelling adventure that captivates imaginations and leaves a lasting impact.

Developing Compelling Beats in Archplot Structure

Beats, as we have established, are the individual moments or turning points in a story that contribute to the overall narrative arc. However, there is much more to creating impactful beats than meets the eye. Let's explore the intricacies of beat development, and uncover techniques to captivate and engage readers on a profound level.

<u>Understanding the Importance of Beats</u>: Beats are not mere structural elements; they are the heartbeat of your story. They breathe life into your characters, propel the plot forward, and evoke powerful emotions within your readers. Each beat should serve as a mini-narrative in itself, with a clear objective and an emotional impact. By understanding the significance of beats, you can leverage their potential to grip readers and keep them invested in your story.

Identifying Key Beats in Your Story:

While major beats like the inciting incident, midpoint, and climax form the primary structural pillars, it is vital to dissect your story further to identify additional key beats that enhance its depth and resonance. Consider moments of internal conflict, personal identity revelations, moral dilemmas, or transformative experiences for your characters. By recognizing these secondary beats, you can add layers of complexity that elevate your story and engage readers on a more intellectual and emotional level.

<u>Determining Beat Placement:</u> Like the rhythm of a well-composed symphony, the placement of beats within your story is paramount to keeping your readers mesmerized. Understand the ebb and flow of your narrative, and ensure that each beat is strategically positioned for maximum impact. Intersperse moments of high tension and action with quieter beats that provide reflection, allowing readers to process the emotions they have experienced. Experiment with the pacing and placement of beats to create a masterful composition that keeps readers on the edge of their seats.

Crafting Engaging Beats: Creating captivating beats requires finesse and insight into the human experience. A beat should be more than just a plot point; it should resonate deeply with readers and elicit an emotional response. Engage all senses to immerse readers in the moment, utilizing vivid descriptions, evocative language, and atmospheric cues to transport them to the heart of your story. Make the conflicts personal and relatable, allowing readers to empathize with the characters and feel their triumphs and tribulations.

Connecting Beats Seamlessly: The fluidity of your narrative relies on the seamless connection between beats. Each beat should serve as a natural progression from the previous one, creating a sense of inevitability while still surprising readers at key moments. Employ subtle foreshadowing and clever setup to interweave beats, creating a sense of interconnectedness that deepens the overall impact. Ensure that the consequences of each beat ripple through the story, affecting subsequent beats and driving the plot forward.

Evolving Beats Through Revision:

The development of beats is an iterative process that demands critical evaluation and revision. Once you have established the core beats, revisit each one with a discerning eye. Ask yourself if the beat fulfills its purpose within the story. Are there opportunities to heighten the conflict, reveal deeper layers of character, or amplify the thematic resonance? Look for ways to refine and strengthen each beat, removing any elements that detract from the overall narrative impact. Be open to experimentation and willing to redefine beats that may not be serving the story as effectively as envisioned. By dedicating time and care to the development of beats within Archplot structure, you can create a narrative that resonates deeply with your readers. Remember to experiment, revise, and refine your beats, allowing them to intensify the impact and captivate the hearts and minds of your audience. The beauty of beat development lies in its ability to surpass the boundaries of structure and touch the very essence of human experience, leaving an indelible mark on the audience's soul.

Unleashing the Power of Conflict and Tension

Conflict and tension are two crucial elements that drive the narrative forward and keep readers engaged in your story. They create opportunities for character development, plot advancement, and emotional resonance. Let's delve into the various aspects of conflict and tension and explore how to effectively unleash their power in your writing.

Types of Conflict: Conflict lies at the heart of storytelling, and understanding the different types can enrich your narrative.

Internal Conflict: Internal conflict occurs within a character's mind and emotions.

It is a battle of conflicting desires, fears, or moral dilemmas. This type of conflict adds depth to your protagonist, allowing readers to witness their inner struggles and personal growth. By exploring the complexity of your characters' internal conflicts, you can create a rich and relatable narrative. Internal conflicts often revolve around choices between competing values or desires. They can manifest as characters grappling with their past mistakes, battling their insecurities or doubts, or dealing with conflicting loyalties. These conflicts create relatable tension, as readers empathize with characters torn between difficult decisions. To effectively portray internal conflict, delve into your characters' thoughts, desires, and fears.

Use introspective scenes, internal monologues, or flashbacks to reveal their inner turmoil. By highlighting the emotional journey of your characters, you invite readers to engage with their struggles and invest in their personal growth.

External Conflict: External conflict is the clash between characters, groups, or forces beyond the control of the protagonist. It can manifest in various forms listed below.

Physical Conflict: This entails physical confrontations, fights, or battles. It raises the stakes and injects adrenaline into the narrative, captivating readers with action-packed scenes. Physical conflict can range from primal hand-to-hand combat to epic battles between armies. By describing the choreography, the impact of blows, and the tactical maneuvers, you immerse readers in the heart-pounding action.

<u>Emotional Conflict</u>: Emotional conflict arises when characters experience deep-seated disagreements, and even misunderstandings, or clashes of values. This type of conflict engages readers' empathy and allows for exploration of complex relationships and interpersonal dynamics. By delving into characters' emotional landscapes, you uncover the underlying tensions that fuel their conflicts. Show conflicting beliefs, hidden agendas, or long-standing resentments to create gripping emotional conflicts.

Ideological Conflict: Ideological conflict stems from differing beliefs, opinions, or ideologies. It presents opportunities to explore themes such as politics, religion, or social issues, fostering thought-provoking conversations and adding intellectual depth to your work. Ideological conflicts can be external, pitting characters against one another, or they can be internal, as a character battles conflicting belief systems within themselves. By respectfully presenting opposing viewpoints and carefully crafting arguments, you encourage readers to reflect on their own perspectives and engage with the themes you present.

Creating Tension: Tension keeps readers on the edge of their seats, eagerly turning the pages to discover the resolution. Here are some techniques to heighten tension in your writing:

Goal-Obstacle Dynamics: The pursuit of a goal becomes all the more compelling when obstacles and challenges arise. These hurdles can test your characters' skills, resilience, and determination, creating tension by raising doubts about their success. Whether it's a formidable antagonist, a series of setbacks, or a mysterious puzzle to solve, obstacles drive the narrative forward while adding layers of tension.

To create effective goal-obstacle dynamics, establish clear goals for your characters early on. Make these goals personal, emotional, and relatable to your readers. Then, introduce obstacles that are difficult, unexpected, and threaten the characters' progress. These obstacles can be external, such as a powerful enemy or a natural disaster, or internal, such as self-doubt or conflicting motivations. As the story progresses, increase the complexity and intensity of the obstacles. Force characters to make difficult choices, confront their fears, or sacrifice their values to overcome obstacles. By showcasing their determination in the face of adversity, you heighten tension and create a satisfying payoff when goals are achieved.

Time Constraint: Introduce time pressure to intensify the sense of urgency. A ticking clock sets characters against a finite timeline, creating tension as they strive to meet their objectives before time runs out. This constraint can create a race against time scenario, heightening stress and forcing characters to make difficult decisions under pressure. To effectively incorporate time constraints, establish the importance of the task or the consequences of failure within the narrative.

Use countdowns, deadlines, or timers to create a tangible sense of urgency. As the deadline approaches, ramp up the tension by presenting unexpected obstacles or complications that hinder the characters' progress. This time constraint will create an atmosphere of suspense, urging readers to keep turning the pages to find out if the characters can beat the clock.

<u>Foreshadowing:</u> Foreshadowing plants subtle hints or indications of future conflicts or events within the narrative. This technique creates anticipation and an underlying unease in readers, building suspense and tension as they eagerly await the resolution of these hinted events. Carefully woven foreshadowing adds a layer of depth to your storytelling and keeps readers engaged. To utilize foreshadowing effectively, begin by identifying key moments or turning points in your story. These moments can include dramatic reveals, major conflicts, or unexpected plot twists. Incorporate subtle clues or symbolic elements earlier in the narrative that hint at these future events. These clues can be visual, like a recurring object or a symbolic image, or they can be verbal, with characters remarking on a feeling or a premonition. By skillfully implanting these hints, you sow seeds of tension and curiosity in readers, enhancing the overall impact of your storytelling.

<u>Conflict Resolution:</u> Conflict resolution is a critical aspect of storytelling that determines the overall impact and satisfaction readers derive from your work.

a. <u>Escalation:</u> As the story progresses, conflicts should gradually escalate in intensity. Raising the stakes and increasing risks heightens the tension and maintains reader engagement. Escalation can involve worsening consequences, higher personal sacrifices, or unexpected revelations that drive the characters toward a climactic confrontation. Effective conflict escalation requires careful plotting and pacing. Begin with smaller conflicts or obstacles that serve as catalysts for larger and more impactful conflicts. Each resolved conflict should create a ripple effect, revealing new layers of conflict and heightening the stakes. As the climax approaches, introduce the highest stakes yet, forcing characters to confront their biggest fears or make their most challenging decisions.

b. <u>Subverting Expectations</u>: Surprise your readers by subverting their expectations when resolving conflicts. This unexpected twist injects a fresh energy into the narrative, shattering predictability and creating heightened tension. Subverting expectations challenges readers' assumptions and keeps them eagerly guessing about the outcomes, resulting in a more gripping and rewarding reading experience.

To effectively subvert expectations, analyze the narrative patterns and conventional resolutions typically found in your genre. Once you understand these expectations, strategically deviate from them in a way that feels organic and true to your story. This unexpected twist can range from a character's unexpected change of heart, an unforeseen alliance formed, or a sudden reversal of fortune. By defying readers' expectations, you create tension and anticipation

c. <u>Character Growth and Transformation</u>: Conflict resolution should also result in meaningful character growth and transformation. As conflicts are resolved, characters should learn valuable lessons, overcome their flaws, and evolve as individuals. This growth adds depth and emotional resonance to your narrative, providing a satisfying closure for readers. To portray character growth effectively, consider the arc of your protagonist and how each conflict shapes their journey.

Show the impact of conflicts on their beliefs, values, and behaviors. Characters should confront their flaws, face their fears, and make difficult choices to overcome obstacles. By showcasing their arc, you give readers a sense of closure and fulfillment, leaving them with a lasting impression.

d. Balance and Closure: Ultimately, conflict resolution should aim for a sense of balance and closure. While not every conflict needs a neat, happy ending, providing closure to significant storylines and character arcs is essential. This closure can include the resolution of major conflicts, the tying up of loose ends, and the fulfillment of character goals. To create a satisfying sense of closure, identify the key conflicts and storylines that require resolution.

Devote sufficient time and attention to these resolutions to ensure reader satisfaction. Address unanswered questions, provide explanations, or offer resolutions that align with the narrative's themes and messages. By delivering a sense of closure, you leave readers with a feeling of fulfillment and completion.

Conflict and tension are powerful tools in storytelling that propel the narrative forward, engage readers, and create meaningful experiences. By understanding the different types of conflict, creating tension through goal-obstacle dynamics, time constraints, and foreshadowing, and resolving conflicts in a satisfying and meaningful way, you can unleash the power of conflict and tension in your writing. Experiment with these techniques, and allow them to shape your narrative into a captivating journey for your readers.

Mastering Plot and Subplots in Archplot Structure

Plot and subplots are essential elements in crafting a compelling and well-rounded story within the Archplot structure. In this section, we will delve deeper into the intricacies of designing and executing a captivating plot that serves as the backbone of your narrative, and explore how subplots can enhance the overall storytelling experience.

The main plot of your Archplot should revolve around the hero's journey, presenting a clear goal or objective that they must pursue throughout the story. This primary storyline should be well-defined, with a beginning, middle, and end, ensuring a satisfying narrative arc. The journey of the hero should be filled with conflicts, obstacles, and moments of personal growth that contribute to their ultimate transformation and resolution.

Within the main plot, it is crucial to establish a series of escalating conflicts that continually challenge the hero's progress, creating tension and suspense. These conflicts can take various forms, such as external obstacles like rivalries, antagonists, or natural disasters, or internal obstacles like doubts, fears, or internal struggles. However, a well-crafted Archplot also incorporates subplots that complement the main plotline.

Subplots provide additional layers of complexity and richness to the story, offering opportunities for character development, thematic exploration, and suspenseful twists. These secondary storylines should intertwine with the main plot in a way that enhances the overall narrative, rather than distracting or overpowering it. When designing subplots, it is crucial to ensure that they are relevant and contribute to the central story in a meaningful way. Each subplot should have its own distinctive narrative arc, complete with its own set of conflicts and resolutions. These subplots should also connect to the main plotline, either by directly impacting the hero's journey or by thematically resonating with the central themes and motifs of the story.

Subplots can serve various purposes within the overall narrative structure. They can provide insight into supporting characters, allowing readers to witness their own personal growth and struggles. These subplots can function as parallel journeys, intersecting and influencing the hero's journey in essential ways. They can also provide subtext and depth, exploring thematic elements or presenting contrasting perspectives that enrich the overall storytelling experience.

To master the art of plot and subplots in Archplot structure, consider the following tips:

1. Establish a clear hierarchy: The main plot should always take precedence, while subplots should serve to enhance and support it. Avoid overcrowding your story with too many subplots, as this can dilute the impact of the main plotline. Prioritize subplots that directly impact the hero's journey or significantly contribute to the central themes of the story.

2. Utilize subplots for character development: Subplots offer an excellent opportunity to deepen your characters, allowing them to face additional challenges and dilemmas that contribute to their overall growth and transformation. Use subplots strategically to reveal hidden aspects of your

characters' personalities and motivations, creating well-rounded and relatable individuals. Subplots can also help showcase the relationships between characters, highlighting tensions, alliances, or friendships that affect both the main plot and subplots.

3. Connect subplots thematically: Find ways to tie the subplots thematically to the main plotline. Identify common motifs, themes, or ideas that can be explored through the subplots, adding depth and resonance to your narrative. This thematic resonance creates a sense of cohesion and unity throughout the story, allowing readers to see the interconnectedness of various storylines. It also provides an opportunity for you, as the

writer, to explore multiple perspectives on a central idea or theme, enriching the overall thematic exploration.

4. Manage pacing and timing: Ensure that the pacing of your main plot and subplots is balanced and harmonized. While the main plot typically drives the story's momentum, subplots can offer moments of respite or additional tension. Consider the placement of subplots strategically, using them to provide breaks from the intensity of the main plot or to heighten the overall tension of the story. Skillful manipulation of pacing and timing can keep readers engaged from chapter to chapter, eager to discover how both the main plot and subplots progress.

5. Resolve subplots effectively: Just as the main plot should have a satisfying resolution, subplots should also reach a conclusive end. Avoid leaving loose ends or unresolved subplots, as this can lead to reader dissatisfaction or confusion. Tie up all loose threads and ensure that each subplot contributes to the overall resolution of the story. However, refrain from delivering predictable or excessively neat resolutions to subplots; instead, aim for resolutions that feel natural and justified within the context of each subplot.

6. Explore different types of subplots: There are various types of subplots you can incorporate into your Archplot structure.

These include romantic subplots that add a layer of emotional depth and intimacy, mystery subplots that provide intrigue and suspense, or even thematic subplots that explore different perspectives or subthemes within the larger narrative.

Experiment with different types of subplots to find those that resonate best with your main plotline and contribute organically to the overall story. By mastering the art of plot and subplots in Archplot structure, you can create a multi-dimensional and captivating story that keeps readers hooked from beginning to end. The careful integration and execution of subplots will elevate your narrative, offering depth, complexity, and a more immersive storytelling experience. With a solid main plot and thoughtfully designed subplots, you can create a rich tapestry of interconnected narratives that leave a lasting impact on your readers.

Building Complex and Believable Antagonists

In every great story, the protagonist needs a formidable adversary to overcome. The antagonist plays a crucial role in driving the conflict and creating tension within the narrative. Building complex and believable antagonists that challenge the protagonist while creating a sense of intrigue and depth can greatly enhance the overall quality of your book.

Motivation: Just like a well-developed protagonist, your antagonist should have a clear and compelling motivation for their actions. A strong and believable motivation will help readers understand their choices and actions, even if they may not agree with them. Consider what drives your antagonist on a deep emotional level. Are they seeking power, control, or personal gain? Do they have a sense of injustice or a desire for revenge? Or are they acting out of a misguided sense of righteousness? By understanding what truly motivates your antagonist, you can better shape their actions and reactions throughout the story. Consider how their motivation aligns or clashes with the goals of your protagonist. This will not only create a strong conflict but also allow readers to understand the antagonist's perspective.

Backstory: A well-developed antagonist has a rich and meaningful backstory that informs their choices and behavior. Delving into their past can provide insights into their fears, insecurities, or resentments, making them feel like a fully realized character. Consider their upbringing, experiences, and the events that shaped their worldview. What major events or traumas have they experienced that have influenced who they have become? How have their past relationships or the dynamics within their family shaped their values and beliefs? Understanding these elements of their backstory will lend authenticity to your antagonist and make them more relatable to readers, even if they don't agree with their actions.

Complexity: Avoid creating one-dimensional villains who are purely evil. Instead, strive to add layers of complexity to your antagonist's character. Show different facets of their personality, conflicting emotions, or moments of vulnerability. By humanizing your antagonist, you create a more engaging and believable character that readers can invest in. Explore the gray areas in their morality, showcasing shades of good and evil. Consider moments where they question their own actions or show remorse, offering glimpses of a redeeming quality. This complexity will make your antagonist feel more authentic and multidimensional, allowing readers to understand the complexities of human nature.

<u>Flaws and Vulnerabilities</u>: Just like your protagonist, your antagonist should have flaws and vulnerabilities that can be exploited. These weaknesses can be physical, emotional, or psychological. By highlighting their vulnerabilities, you create opportunities for your protagonist to outsmart or defeat them, adding depth and tension to the story. Show how their flaws hinder them in their pursuit of their goals and how these vulnerabilities can become their downfall. This not only creates opportunities for plot developments but also reinforces the humanity and relatability of your antagonist. No one is perfect, and by showcasing the flaws and vulnerabilities of your antagonist, you make them more realistic and relatable.

Counterbalance: Consider creating an antagonist who serves as a counterbalance to your protagonist. This could be through contrasting personality traits, beliefs, or methods. The dynamic between your protagonist and antagonist should be a battle of equals, pushing each other to their limits and forcing growth on both sides. Explore how their differences impact their interactions and the choices they make. This counterbalance can also serve as a reflection of the central conflict in your story, highlighting the opposing forces at play. By creating a strong counterbalance, you increase the stakes and make the conflict more compelling for readers.

Subtlety and Nuance: Avoid creating a caricature of evil. Instead, focus on subtle nuances in your antagonist's behavior and dialogue. Show moments of humanity or conflicting emotions that make them more multi-dimensional. Adding subtlety and nuance to your antagonist will make them feel more realistic. Consider small gestures, facial expressions, or internal thoughts that reveal deeper layers to their personality. Pay attention to their speech patterns and the way they interact with others. Do they have a particular way of convincing or manipulating others?

This attention to detail will greatly enrich their character and make them stand out in readers' minds.

<u>Parallel Character Arcs:</u> Consider creating parallels or mirror images between your protagonist and antagonist's character arcs. This can involve exploring similar themes, desires, or internal struggles. By doing so, you create a deeper connection between the two characters and highlight their shared humanity. Reflect on how they both undergo personal growth and transformation throughout the story. Are there moments where they face similar challenges or make similar choices? This parallelism can create an emotional resonance and demonstrate that the antagonist is not merely an obstacle, but someone who is also grappling with their own journey.

<u>Foils and Complex Relationships</u>: A strong antagonist can be further developed by exploring their relationships with other characters in the story. Consider their interactions with allies, subordinates, or even potential love interests. How do these relationships reveal different aspects of your antagonist's character? Do they have loyal followers, or does their behavior alienate those around them? These complex relationships can provide further depth to your antagonist and add layers to their motivations and actions. It can also create opportunities for unexpected alliances or betrayals within the narrative.

Remember, a well-crafted antagonist is just as important as a compelling protagonist in driving the narrative forward. Building complex and believable antagonists will elevate your book, providing readers with a captivating and immersive reading experience. By exploring their motivations, backstory, complexity, flaws, vulnerabilities, counterbalance, subtlety, parallel character arcs, and complex relationships, you can create a truly memorable antagonist that leaves a lasting impact on your readers.

Incorporating Theme and Symbolism in Archplot Structure

Themes and symbolism form the backbone of a story, infusing it with depth and resonance. These narrative elements transcend the surface-level plot, connecting readers to universal truths and inviting contemplation. Let's explore advanced techniques and strategies for effectively incorporating theme and symbolism in Archplot structure, delving deeper into their profound impact on storytelling.

<u>Understanding Theme:</u> A theme serves as the guiding principle of a story, embodying its core concepts and universal messages. To incorporate theme into your Archplot structure, it is crucial to elevate it beyond a mere backdrop. Instead, treat the theme as a living entity, allowing it to influence every aspect of the narrative, from character development to plot progression. By consciously immersing your story in the essence of your chosen theme, you create a cohesive and powerful experience for your readers. To deepen your exploration of theme, consider weaving it through various layers of the narrative. Show how it impacts not only the central characters but also the peripheral ones, highlighting its far-reaching consequences. Moreover, reflect the theme in the setting, atmosphere, and tone of the story. A well-executed theme saturates the entire world you create, engrossing readers and immersing them in its intricate web of ideas and emotions.

Symbolism: Symbolism breathes life into a story, adding layers of meaning and evoking profound emotions. Each symbol acts as a gateway, opening doors to hidden realms of understanding. To harness the power of symbolism in your Archplot structure, consider employing both overt and subtle symbols. Overt symbols anchor readers, providing clear signposts and enhancing comprehension. In contrast, subtle symbols, like whispers carried on the wind, invite readers to embark on their personal journey of discovery within your narrative. Authentic symbolism emerges from careful consideration of each element's associations, cultural significance, and metaphorical potential. Unearth archetypal symbols that resonate on a collective, timeless level. Leverage cultural symbols to evoke specific emotions, memories, or beliefs. Pay attention to multisensory symbolism, employing vivid descriptions that appeal to readers' senses and deepen their connection to the story's themes. By seamlessly infusing symbolism into the fabric of your Archplot structure, you create an exquisite tapestry of meaning, enriching the reader's experience.

Consistency and Integration: To realize the full impact of theme and symbolism, consistency and integration are paramount. The theme must permeate every word, every action, and every choice made by your characters. It should be the invisible hand guiding their growth, challenges, and interactions. By integrating the theme intrinsically, you unify all narrative elements, ensuring that they converge and harmonize. Consistency and integration extend to symbolism as well. Each symbol must serve the greater purpose of the theme, reinforcing and expanding its implications. Integrate recurring symbols throughout the story, revealing their evolving meanings and fostering a sense of connection between them. Employ motifs to underscore key moments, reflecting the theme's resonance in the reader's subconscious mind. Embracing consistency and integration, your Archplot structure becomes a vessel that skillfully carries readers through a transformative journey.

<u>Subtle vs. Overt</u>: The interplay between subtle and overt symbolism infuses your story with nuance and intrigue. Subtle symbolism invites readers to engage actively, unraveling hidden meanings beneath a veil of subtlety. It stirs their curiosity, inviting them to immerse themselves fully in your world and encourages deeper reflection. Overt symbolism, on the other hand, serves as a beacon, illuminating specific themes and guiding readers' understanding. It provides clarity and direction, ensuring that your intended message is received effectively. Strike a balance between subtlety and overt representation, considering the needs and preferences of your intended readership. Experiment with blending the two, layering symbols to create a multifaceted and engaging experience. By intertwining subtle and overt symbolism, you create a compelling tension that fosters exploration and introspection.

The Power of Contrast: Contrasting elements serve as a potent tool to explore the complexities of human experiences and deepen thematic exploration. By juxtaposing opposing ideas, symbols, or personalities, you invite readers to confront contradictions and navigate the intricate shades of gray that shape our lives. Contrasts enhance the impact of your themes and symbolism, amplifying their resonance and challenging readers' beliefs and preconceptions. Introduce conflicts that embody contrasting values and beliefs, forcing characters to confront their own biases and growth. Vividly illustrate these conflicts through dynamic scenes, revealing the inherent tension within issues central to your theme. Through these moments of contrasting symbolism, you open doors to deeper understanding and encourage readers to embrace the duality inherent in all aspects of the human condition.

Layered Symbolism: Depth and complexity can be achieved by employing layered symbolism, where multiple symbols intersect and interact, enhancing the theme's impact. Each layer represents a distinct facet of the theme, individually significant, but collectively presenting a nuanced exploration of your message. By interweaving these symbols, you invite readers to engage within a rich tapestry of meaning and interpretations. Ensure that each layer of symbolism harmonizes with the overarching theme, amplifying its message rather than diluting it. As symbols intersect and collide, explore the tensions and connections arising from their convergence. Use the interplay of these symbols to mirror the intricacies of your characters' development, relationships, and struggles, emphasizing the profound interconnection between individual experiences and universal truths.

When incorporating theme and symbolism into your Archplot structure, embrace the transformative potential of these narrative elements. Allow your chosen theme to permeate every corner of your story, encompassing characters, plot, and setting. Infuse your symbolism with profound thought and intention, selecting symbols that resonate deeply with readers. By carefully balancing subtlety and overt representation, weaving contrasting elements, and exploring layered symbolism, you create a narrative that resonates on a universal level, leaving an indelible mark in the hearts and minds of your readers.

Polishing and Perfecting Your Archplot Manuscript

Now, let's examine the essential steps and strategies for polishing and perfecting your Archplot manuscript. While the writing process is undoubtedly creative and exciting, the revision and editing stage is equally crucial to elevate your story to its fullest potential. First, let's explore key aspects to consider and practical techniques to make your manuscript shine.

Revisiting the Big Picture: Before diving into the nitty-gritty details, take a step back and evaluate your manuscript as a whole. This macro-level assessment will help you identify the strengths and weaknesses of your story. Consider the overall structure, pacing, and flow of the narrative. Are there any pacing inconsistencies or sections that feel sluggish? Are there moments where the tension could be heightened?

Analyze the story arc and make sure that it follows a logical progression with smooth transitions between acts and scenes. Look for any gaps or unresolved plot points that need addressing. Ensure that the central conflict remains compelling and tension is sustained throughout the narrative, maintaining your readers' interest. This big-picture evaluation will help you identify areas of improvement and set the stage for a focused revision.

Strengthening Character Development:

Characters are the heart and soul of any story. Take a closer look at your protagonist and supporting characters. Are their motivations clear and consistent throughout the story? Do they have unique and well-defined personalities that make them memorable? Dive deep into their backgrounds, identify their fears, hopes, and desires, and explore their emotional journey. Ensure their actions and decisions align with their established traits and backgrounds, creating believable and relatable character arcs. Eliminate any unnecessary or inconsistent character traits that may detract from their authenticity. Aim to create multidimensional individuals that resonate with your readers. Give your characters room to evolve and grow, allowing them to face internal conflicts and transform throughout the story, making them more relatable and engaging.

<u>Streamlining Dialogue</u>: Dialogue plays a crucial role in bringing your characters to life and advancing the plot. Make sure your dialogue is natural, authentic, and purposeful. Avoid overly expository or on-the-nose conversations that spell out information for the reader. Each line of dialogue should serve a specific purpose, whether it be revealing character traits, advancing the plot, or creating tension. Use dialogue tags sparingly and favor strong action beats and subtext to enhance the impact of your conversations. Experiment with different dialogue techniques, such as witty banter, thoughtful monologues, or poignant exchanges, to add depth and complexity to your character interactions. Additionally, consider the individual voices and speaking styles of your characters, ensuring they are distinct and reflective of their personality and background. This attention to dialogue will make your characters feel alive and your story more engaging.

<u>Sharpening Descriptive Writing</u>: Descriptive writing allows readers to visualize and immerse themselves in your story's world.

As you polish your manuscript, take a closer look at your descriptions and elevate them with vivid and sensory language. Paint detailed pictures in your readers' minds by incorporating the five senses—sight, sound, smell, taste, and touch. Strike a balance between providing enough detail to create a rich visual experience without overwhelming readers with excessive information.

Show, don't tell, by using specific details, active verbs, and engaging metaphors or similes. This will create a more immersive experience for your readers, making them feel like they are part of your story's world. Embrace the power of evocative imagery to transport your readers to vibrant settings and evoke strong emotions. Descriptive writing done right not only engages your readers but also deepens their emotional connection to the story.

<u>Editing for Clarity and Consistency</u>:

As you polish your manuscript, pay close attention to clarity and consistency. Review your sentences and paragraphs for clarity of meaning, eliminating any ambiguity or awkward phrasing. Ensure that your writing style remains consistent throughout the manuscript, avoiding sudden shifts in tone, tense, or perspective that can be jarring to your readers. Inconsistencies in names, dates, or other details can disrupt the reader's immersion, so create a system for tracking and verifying these elements. Take note of recurring phrases, words, or stylistic devices to maintain thematic coherence and enhance the overall reading experience. Aim for a harmonious balance between lyrical prose and streamlined storytelling, allowing your unique voice to shine through while maintaining clear and coherent communication. Remember, clarity and consistency contribute to a seamless reading experience that keeps your audience engaged.

Seeking Feedback: One of the most valuable resources during the polishing stage is feedback from trusted beta readers or writing critique groups. Share your manuscript with others and encourage them to provide honest and constructive feedback. Consider their perspectives while remaining true to your vision. Use their insights to identify areas of improvement that may have been overlooked and make necessary revisions accordingly. Pay attention to recurring patterns in the feedback and address common concerns or criticisms. This collaborative process will enhance your manuscript, uncovering blind spots and strengthening weak areas. Be open to constructive criticism, as it will ultimately help you create a more well-rounded and impactful story. However, also remember to trust your instincts and make sure that any changes align with your overall vision for the story.

The Proofreading Process: Once you are satisfied with the overall structure and content of your manuscript, it's time for a meticulous proofreading process. While proofreading involves searching for grammatical errors, typos, or punctuation mistakes, it goes beyond surface-level corrections. Carefully examine each sentence, word choice, and punctuation mark to ensure clarity, coherence, and precision. Scan for inconsistencies in formatting, such as the use of italics or quotation marks. Double-check that your manuscript adheres to industry-standard guidelines for font size, line spacing, and margins.

Pay attention to proper grammar usage, punctuation, and sentence structure, refining your writing for readability and impact. Taking the time to carefully proofread your manuscript will help you present a polished and professional final product that reflects your dedication to excellence. Remember, the process of polishing and perfecting your Archplot manuscript may require multiple iterations and rounds of revision. Embrace the feedback and take the time necessary to refine your work to the best of your ability. With patience, dedication, and a commitment to quality, your manuscript will emerge as a visual and compelling story that captivates readers and leaves a lasting impact.

Archplot Structure and its Significance in Storytelling

Let's review the fundamental elements of Archplot, including the three-act structure, plot points, and the importance of a clear beginning, middle, and end. Take note of how Archplot structure helps create a more compelling narrative arc and keeps readers engaged throughout the story.

Archplot Structure: A Foundation for Compelling Storytelling

Archplot structure, also referred to as the classical narrative structure, provides a roadmap for crafting a compelling and coherent story. It consists of three major acts: setup, confrontation, and resolution. Each act has specific purposes and milestones that propel the narrative forward and captivate readers.

The Three Acts:

Setup, Confrontation, & Resolution

<u>Act 1</u>: **<u>The Setup</u>** The setup introduces the readers to the story's world, characters, and conflict. It sets the stage for the upcoming events and establishes the narrative's central premise. The setup typically includes the exposition, which provides essential information about the story's setting, characters, and their relationships. Within the setup, the inciting incident occurs, which disrupts the protagonist's ordinary world and sets them on their journey. This incident acts as a catalyst, triggering the events that will propel the narrative and create tension and conflict.

It is essential for the inciting incident to be clear and engaging, so readers are immediately hooked into the story. However, a well-crafted setup goes beyond mere information dumping. It finds ways to engage the readers by introducing intriguing characters, establishing a unique setting, or presenting a compelling conflict. Through engaging dialogue, vivid descriptions, and immersive world-building, the setup entices readers to invest their time and emotions into the story.

Act 2: The Confrontation The confrontation is the longest act and constitutes the core of the story. It is where the protagonist faces increasingly difficult challenges, and the tension and stakes rise. The second act is often divided into two parts: the rising action and the midpoint. The rising action encompasses a series of obstacles and conflicts that the protagonist must overcome. It should introduce complications and raise the stakes, driving the story forward and engaging readers.

Plot points, which are pivotal moments in the narrative, occur during this phase. The first plot point, also known as the point of no return, usually happens toward the end of the first act or the beginning of the second act. It presents a significant change or revelation that propels the story forward and heightens the conflict. However, the rising action should not simply be a random series of events. It needs to be carefully crafted to maintain a sense of narrative coherence and progression. Each obstacle or conflict should build upon the previous one, increasing in intensity and complexity. As the protagonist navigates through these challenges, their character should undergo growth and transformation, allowing readers to connect with their journey on a deeper level.

The midpoint, often referred to as the climax of Act 2, is a crucial turning point in the story. It deepens the conflict and often reveals unexpected twists or revelations. This pivotal moment creates a shift in the narrative and propels the protagonist toward the story's climax.

Act 3: The Resolution The resolution is the final act of the Archplot structure, where the story reaches its climax and wraps up loose ends. The climax is the culmination of the protagonist's journey and represents the peak of tension, conflict, and emotional intensity. It often involves the ultimate confrontation between the protagonist and the antagonist, where their goals and motivations collide.

A compelling resolution involves more than just tying up loose ends. It should provide a sense of catharsis or closure for readers. The resolution should address the narrative's central conflicts, resolve character arcs, and deliver on the promises made throughout the story. It may include moments of emotional payoff, where the protagonist's growth and transformation are fully realized, leaving readers with a deeply satisfying sense of fulfillment.

Following the climax, the story enters the denouement, also known as the falling action. This phase provides closure by resolving any remaining conflicts and tying up loose ends. It allows readers to reflect on the journey and the transformation the protagonist has undergone. However, the denouement shouldn't be rushed or overly prolonged. It should strike a balance between tying up loose ends and giving readers a chance to process the story's events. By providing a conclusion that feels earned and meaningful, the denouement leaves a lasting impact and ensures a satisfying reading experience.

The Importance of a Clear Beginning, Middle, & End

The Archplot structure's emphasis on a clear beginning, middle, and end is essential for creating a satisfying narrative. A strong beginning hooks readers, establishes the story's premise, and introduces compelling characters. It sets up the conflicts and stakes that will drive the story forward. However, a clear beginning doesn't mean that everything needs to be laid out in a straightforward manner. It's essential to find the right balance between exposition and mystery, providing enough information to engage readers while leaving room for curiosity and discovery. By piquing readers' curiosity, the beginning sets the stage for the narrative's progression and entices them to continue reading.

The middle, comprising the confrontation, is where the majority of the story unfolds. It is essential to maintain a balance between action, character development, and plot progression to keep readers engaged. The rising action and midpoint provide twists and turns that keep the narrative dynamic and prevent it from becoming predictable or stagnant. However, a well-developed middle is more than just a sequence of thrilling events. It should explore the characters' motivations, fears, and desires, allowing readers to develop a deeper connection with them. By exploring the internal struggles within the characters and the consequences of their actions, the middle creates emotional investment and empathy, making the story resonate on a profound level.

The end brings resolution and closure to the story. A well-crafted resolution allows readers to reflect on the protagonist's journey, the themes explored, and the lessons learned. It leaves a lasting impact and ensures a satisfying reading experience. However, a satisfying ending doesn't mean everything has to be wrapped up neatly. It can leave room for interpretation, allowing readers to contemplate the story's deeper meanings or invite them to imagine what happens next. By striking the right balance between resolution and ambiguity, the ending lingers in readers' minds, leaving them with a sense of wonder and contemplation.

Adapting Archplot Structure to Different Genres

While the Archplot structure applies to a wide range of storytelling genres, it is essential to adapt it to suit the specific needs and conventions of each genre. For example, mystery novels may involve more intricate plot twists and red herrings, while romance stories may heavily focus on the development of the central characters' relationship. By understanding the unique expectations and elements of different genres, writers can effectively utilize the Archplot structure and create compelling narratives tailored to their chosen genre.

Archplot structure provides a tried-and-tested foundation for crafting compelling stories. Understanding and applying its elements, such as the three-act structure, plot points, and clear beginning, middle, and end, enables writers to create engaging narratives that captivate readers from start to finish. By incorporating Archplot structure into their storytelling toolbox, writers can build powerful narratives that resonate with audiences and stand the test of time.

About the Author

Michelle Murray is an author, screenwriter, thought leader, and advocate for servant leadership and personal development. Throughout her career in the United States Army and then leading her subsequent teams over a span of three decades, Michelle has endeavored to inspire individuals to discover their true potential, lead with compassion, and make a positive impact on the world around them.

Michelle Murray is a native Texan. She is a combat Veteran of the United States Army. She held a variety of leadership assignments as an Air Defense Soldier, including being a test candidate for the Stinger Missile program when consideration was given to opening it up to women, and she was one of the only female Air Defense Artillery Soldiers to jump with the Golden Knights. She also served as the Brigade Adjutant for the world's largest Air Defense Artillery Brigade, the 11th Air Defense Artillery Brigade.

Prior to a career in the United States Army, Michelle was a member of the Ft Worth Police Department's Weed and Seed Division, an arm of the federal drug task force of the same name. She had the pleasure of also being a part of the department's Kid's Code Blue Program, a program which helped rehabilitate juvenile offenders and provide opportunities to at-risk youth. Additionally, a fun fact is that she mentored thousands of elementary aged children while working as the mascot McGruff the crime dog.

In addition to being COO of KMP Entertainment, she enjoys hobbies that include: SCUBA Diving, camping, hiking, horse-back riding, a few sports, and extensive travel, and spending time with her son.

Her most recent novels are available in both e-book and traditional formats wherever books are sold.

Michelle's resume credits also include Fox's The Cleaning Lady, Will Smith's Netflix movie "Bright", and Season One, Episode 13 of the CBS show "Man With a Plan," "Crazy Ones," with Robin Williams and "The Mentalist." Additionally, you can follow her on Newsbreak for news delivery that is always based in fact and never emotion.

Also of note, Michelle was the 2019 Ms. North Hollywood title holder for the Ms. California Plus Pageant, and the 2023 Miss California Queen of Charity title holder. She is a Rotarian, and avid community volunteer. Michelle holds a Bachelor degree in Entertainment Business and a Master of Fine

Arts degree in Creative Writing. She is currently wrapping up work on her Doctorate.

Michelle enjoys hearing from readers. You can contact her/give her feedback by emailing her at info@kmpentertainment.org If you would like to review this book, or any of her others, please leave a review on Barnes and Noble, Walmart, Amazon or other retailer pages.

You can keep up with Michelle's projects by going to her company's website www.kmpentertainment.org or via Facebook at the KMP Entertainment page, https://www.facebook.com/KMPEntertainment/